WHERE THE RUBBER MEETS THE ROAD

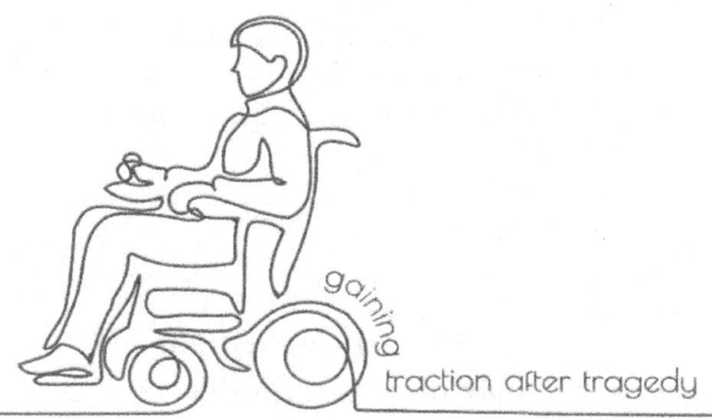

A Memoir of Byron Sellers' Life and Legacy
as told by his wife

SCARLET SELLERS

Disclaimer

These are my personal stories, from my perspective, and I have tried to represent events as faithfully as possible.

Neither the author or the publisher is engaged in rendering professional advice or services to the individual reader.

ISBN: 9798872376903

Editor: Mary Padgett

Publisher: Young's Solutions LLC.

Dedication

I dedicate this book to my beloved husband's amazing parents, Don and Karen Sellers. This book is a tribute to the amazing man you raised, and the endless loving support you gave through many hills and valleys. Ms. Karen - you were his unwavering biggest supporter and loved him unconditionally. Mr. Don - you were the person Byron called when he wanted to talk about sports or get advice. Thank you for sharing him with me for a short while.

I also want to dedicate this book to our children Josie, Janie, and Luoc who continue to carry our family forward with bravery and strength. Thank you for allowing me to share a small piece of our laughter, love, and adventure with others. You were his greatest joy as he strolled through the neighborhood with you, read you his favorite books, or watched you play sports. Dad loved you all very much and I hope this book will be a treasure for you to keep close to your hearts.

I offer this written legacy of love in honor of Byron, who brought me closer to God and was the missing piece that made me complete. Although we couldn't be more different, I was blessed to call him my best friend, husband, adventure seeker, co-parent, and Pu-kin!.

Table of Contents

Chapter ONE

The Mystery Man

Sitting in the back of Sunday school class, I convinced my best friend, Chrystal, to volunteer with me and drive a new classmate to church events. The new guy appeared handsome and smart. His hair was nicely combed, he was well dressed, and his blue eyes were especially handsome. Instead of coming to the back, he sat in the front and made friends. He was chatting and laughing and making small talk. He was attentive to the lesson and gave input throughout the class. As I sat near the back, I caught myself staring at him.

Over the next few weeks, this cute guy wasn't in class, and I didn't see him in church. No one mentioned him from Sunday to Sunday and, according to my astute observations, there was no evidence that he attended any of the weekly class activities. Weeks and months went by, and I found myself at a church ice cream social on a Sunday afternoon in June. I was standing in a circle with friends, just talking and enjoying our ice cream. It surprised me when this same handsome man joined our circle. Everyone continued to talk like he was a typical part of the group and he jumped into the conversation with confidence and ease. We all laughed and talked until he said, "I don't know all of you, so could you tell me your names?" About 8 people were standing around and everyone introduced themselves. We shared our first and last names, and just as I was about to say my last name, he unexpectedly interrupted me and asked, "Scarlet Smith?" It seemed like he already knew who I was.

My heart was pounding as I looked at my best friend in shock. He continued to explain, "I think I saw your name on a contact list that they gave me in case I needed a ride." I was speechless, so Chrystal jumped in to save me, saying, "We signed up together to drive for you." Staring at the ground and giggling nervously, I managed to find my words and added, "But you haven't called!" Thank goodness more people were standing around continuing the conversation because once again I didn't know what to say and I was really nervous. After we all introduced ourselves, he followed up. "It's nice to meet you all. I'm Byron."

As the afternoon continued, I pulled my nerves together enough to engage in the conversation and we all hung out and enjoyed the social. As Byron headed out to another engagement, I noticed how eager I was to meet him and glad he finally came to an event. I questioned my friends to see if they knew anything else about this new mysterious man, but no one had much information to share. I would have to hold on to hope that he would call for a ride to church next Sunday.

Monday night, I was sitting in my condo watching TV, and my phone rang. It was him! I was terrified to answer, but thrilled he called. I answered and tried to play it cool, but his words were so kind as he effortlessly described his call as an opportunity to get to know me better and put a name with a face on a list. We talked about our jobs, families, interests, and our connection to the church. The call lasted 45 minutes, and it turned out to be the most intentional and deliberate conversation I had with an eligible man in quite some time! I distinctly remember lying on the couch and envisioning what this relationship could become.

This would not have been unusual for me, except this cute, friendly guy who had caught my attention was in a wheelchair and appeared to have been paralyzed for some period of time. Strangely enough, as we talked on that first night, his mode of transportation wasn't the focus of our conversation.

Maybe my background as a special education teacher made him comfortable, as he opted not to discuss how he ended up in the chair. That night I learned about his life as a quadriplegic, the challenges of depending on others, and his heart to serve people with disabilities. Our brief conversation turned into a sleepless night for me as I imagined all the hopeful possibilities and prayed he would call again.

It's a Date?

Forty-eight hours later, the same number came up on my caller ID. I answered, hoping he was going to ask for a ride to church that weekend. After another hour of talking about our day and the events of the week, he asked, "Would you be interested in going to lunch on Saturday?" My mind went into immediate panic! Saturday? Lunch? Me? How? What would we talk about? What would I wear? Where would we go? Would I drive? Does he have a car? Really? Why not church on Sunday? I had been eager to see and talk to Byron, even looking forward to driving him to church; however, I never thought he would ask me to lunch. Was this a date? I hadn't been on a date in many months, and I wasn't sure what to say. Eventually, I found my words and responded to his question, "Sure, that would be fun."

As we talked about the logistics of how this lunch was going to take place, Byron's now familiar calming conversational tone made me feel at ease. Before I could ask, he had all my questions answered. He was certain that our lunch would not be ordinary, but he knew we would enjoy it. He went into great detail about the meeting arrangements, including the time and place, leaving my car at his place, and driving a van designed for his wheelchair. Byron made jokes, He made me laugh, and as I would soon come to find out he had a special way of making everyone comfortable around him. As the conversation ended that Wednesday night, we had a plan and date for lunch on

Saturday. He asked if he could call Friday night to confirm and finalize plans. Of course, I wholeheartedly agreed and noticed how polite, thoughtful, and what a gentleman he appeared to be, and he was quite cute too! I looked forward to talking again at the end of the week, but I kept our lunch a secret as I wondered whether it was an actual date or just a friendly meal.

"You Better Get Ready"

Friday came, and we talked again. Saturday came, and I managed to get dressed and drive myself to his house. He was ready and waiting for me and made jokes as I drove up. He immediately engaged in conversation and made me feel comfortable, even though I was terrified. Terrified of driving someone else's car and not just a car, a large, old van and he wasn't in a seatbelt but just holding on. After Byron got in the van and I closed the doors, I went to the driver's seat and noticed his arm slung over the back of the driver's seat. As I thought about it, my fear turned to panic. I am now driving with this paralyzed guy in a wheelchair and I don't even know where I'm going! I had never driven a van this big before, and now his arm was touching my hair, and I was freaking out!

Byron's clear directions, small talk, and jokes along the way continued to make me feel comfortable. At lunch, he was a gentleman, ordering, paying, taking the lead, and answering lots of questions. This kind, caring, and funny man was making his way into my heart over lunch and window shopping. We laughed, talked, and enjoyed each other's company, and I noticed I was no longer nervous in this new situation. During our time, Byron explained why he was in the wheelchair and some of what that meant. He

was absolutely clear that he believed God would provide a wife for him and he was eagerly waiting for that. I replied, "Oh, my sister is an ER nurse, and I don't do 'nurse-y' things like body fluids, or anything involving hospitals and blood or guts." As we parted ways that day, a smile took over my face. I was so happy, and I had a feeling that this was going to be something special.

The next day, Byron headed out of town for work, and I went on a trip with my parent's church. I didn't know if or when I would hear from him again, but I was hopeful and excited about what could come from this friendship. That afternoon, I called my sister to tell her about Byron. I gave her some details but mainly just vague information. I remember telling her, "Renee, he is perfect but in a wheelchair. I am definitely not a nurse, and he can't hike, play ball, or camp with me." My witty sister didn't miss a beat, and replied, "Ha, ha, you better get ready because you just went to lunch with your future husband!" As always, I told her she was crazy and that he would have been a perfect match for her. I told her it was unfair for God to create the perfect man for me, only to have him become a quadriplegic, living his life in a wheelchair. She just laughed and kept repeating, "You better get ready!"

Chapter TWO

Chasing Love

If life were predictable, Byron would have returned from his work trip and called to check in on how my week had gone. Normally, we would catch up with each other, exchange stories, and share how God had worked while we were serving in ministry in two different states. But predictable was not a word that Byron knew well, and I was gradually realizing how rapidly his life could change.

On Sunday, Byron called and asked how my week was. In Scarlet style, I rattled on about what a great week I had and all the things God did while serving at youth camp. After I talked for about 15 minutes about myself, I asked about his week. His response was the last thing I ever dreamed he would say. "I had a great week. God taught me a lot through the families I was working with, but mostly he taught me to be humble." "Humble?" I asked.

He continued in his casual manner, "Well, at this camp we take people with disabilities and do things you typically do at summer camp. Things like rock climbing, tubing, rafting, and playing paintball. So, since I'm an adventurous guy, I thought I would go rafting and now I'm in the hospital with a broken femur."

Expect the Unexpected

My response was anything but calm. I was freaking out and my mind was running a mile a minute. What do you mean in the hospital? How did you break your femur? You don't even walk. What happens now? My list of thoughts and questions was endless.

This should have been my first sign of Byron's character and dependency on Christ. However, I missed that sign and all I could focus on was that I wouldn't get to go on another date for a long time. I was conflicted about my next move. He didn't offer any information about which hospital he was in or invite me to come to visit. I had known this guy for a whole 10 days. Was that enough time to make a hospital visit? Should I tell someone at church to go see him? I struggled with how to handle this crisis, and Byron was acting like it was no big deal.

After a few long weeks, I took a chance by calling Byron and offering to bring food to the hospital. Everyone has to eat, right? So, even though I loathe hospitals, I called. He must have been having a bad day because he didn't feel like eating or seeing me. I was confused, defeated, mad, and frustrated. I decided that maybe this wasn't God's plan; it was just mine. So I made a promise to myself that I would never call and offer to bring food to him again.

Days went by and he finally called. He called! We chatted briefly, and he nonchalantly mentioned that he would enjoy some food if I wanted to come for a visit. If there's one thing my mama taught me about living in the South, it's that food holds the key to a man's heart. So, we made a plan and soon I was on my way to the hospital with a steak burrito in hand! As soon as I arrived, fear gripped me again and my brain was running crazy. I had no idea what I was walking into, and I was a nervous wreck. My mind was racing with questions like, what would he look like in the hospital? How would he eat this gourmet meal I was about to deliver? How long should I stay?

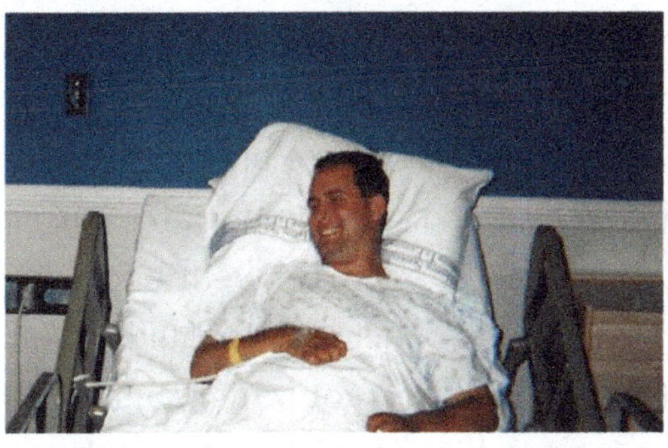

Eventually, I got myself together and walked into the hospital. I found his room and went in, but I truly couldn't speak because I was so scared. Thankfully, Byron still had his calm demeanor and charm and could carry the conversation. He seemed to be a natural at being in the hospital and appeared unphased by all the medical happenings around him. He wasn't concerned about the constant noise of machines, medicines, smells, beds, and nurses. Once I got past all of those things, Byron was still the same fun guy that I had lunch with a few weeks prior. He walked me through how to set up his food so he could eat his steak burrito. I stayed until he was done, cleaned up any evidence that I had been there, and promptly left. I didn't hug him, shake his hand, or make any future plans. His gratitude, humor, and contentment never wavered, despite my discomfort in the hospital. It was truly extraordinary.

The entire way home, I complained and fussed at the Lord about how this whole situation made little sense to me. How did He let this happen? Why would He allow a man with amazing looks and fantastic character to be paralyzed and now have a broken leg? What does that even mean - a broken leg when you can't walk? In all of my nervousness at the hospital, I realized I hadn't even asked about his leg or when he would get out of the hospital. He was undoubtedly thinking about how insensitive and uncaring I appeared. How did I stay in his hospital room for an hour and not even ask about his health? My mind went back over everything I said to him and I concluded I would never hear from him again. Thankfully, Byron got hungry again and called. I could bring food to him again. This time when I got to his hospital room, a woman was sitting in a chair, all comfy and covered with a blanket. It seemed like she had been there for a while and wasn't leaving anytime soon. I immediately felt uncomfortable, as if I was intruding, so I left his food on the bedside table and told him it was great to see him. The visit lasted all of 15 minutes.

My mind was going crazy AGAIN! This time I was SURE I would NEVER hear from him again. Plus, who was this girl? How long had she been there? Did he invite me over, knowing she was there? Was I out of place? I was angry with the Lord. Why did this happen? And why was Byron still in the hospital after 2 months? That seemed to me like an awful long time for a broken leg.

After some soul-searching and advice from my sister, I decided to just call him and ask if I could come visit. She encouraged me to ask questions and gave me a list of questions to ask. So, I followed her suggestion and, as always, Byron welcomed my visit. I asked all my questions, and I learned so much about Byron. The most valuable thing was that he was complex. A broken leg for a quadriplegic person is way more complicated than a broken leg for a person who could walk. The healing process required a unique treatment plan, more than simple surgery or just wearing a cast. This was part of the reason his recovery seemed so slow and why he was still in the hospital after 2 months. Byron continued to be positive and hoped that he would get out of the hospital soon. Although I still had many questions for God about why Byron was going through all of this, I was more hopeful as I left my visit with him that day. Maybe his hope was rubbing off on me.

The next week, when I went for a visit, a man named Mark stopped by while I was there. Unlike the previous visitor, I felt at ease watching them laugh and joke while catching up on life and ministry. I could see their relationship was a strong one, and the time passed quickly. I left with the impression that it was the best hospital visit yet!

For the next few weeks, almost every time I visited Byron, Mark seemed to show up at one point or another. This was helpful for me because I still hated hospitals and I didn't know what to say. All I had to do was stand there, smile, laugh, and answer their questions. I could smoothly be a part of the conversation while finding out more about Byron and his friend Mark. Then, just as this whole "relationship" thing was feeling normal, they released Byron from the hospital. We had built our relationship around food delivery and Mark's visiting schedule, but things were changing and I wasn't sure what that meant.

Two Steps Forward, One Step Back

Over the next few months, I didn't hear from Byron. He didn't come to church; He didn't call, and I didn't know what was happening with him. I was so sad and so worried about him but didn't know how to check on him. What was appropriate at this point? Did he want to talk to me? I confidently concluded that healing and getting better was his priority. I tried to minimize my loneliness and stop thinking about dating, or at least just being his friend with the possibility of dating in the future. There was an unexplainable quality about this man! His crystal blue eyes, welcoming smile, sense of humor, and inner joy embodied the qualities I sought in a husband, yet there was something unique about this guy. Not just because he used a wheelchair and was a quadriplegic, but his character and personality were unlike anyone I had ever known before. I found myself drawn to him, but also wondering why it seemed to be so hard. The Lord would have to make a way if this was His will.

Two weeks before Christmas in 2002, our Sunday School teacher asked us to pray for Byron. He shared with the class that Byron had been at home recovering but had to be taken back to the hospital. He shared little of the details, but my heart sank. All the questions started flooding my brain again. Why had he not called to tell me he was back in the hospital? Isn't that what a friend would do? Were we friends, or had I just convinced myself that this amazing man - who was absolutely perfect in my eyes, truly cared about me? If he was at all interested in me, wouldn't he have called? I felt like a terrible friend and found myself sad and frustrated once again.

As a stubborn individual, I refused to give up on a friendship I believed to be extraordinary. So, since it was Christmas, I decided that he needed a tree or, at minimum, some decorations. I planned to take a tree and decorations over to his house and get it all ready for when he got home from the hospital. Isn't that what any self-respecting "friend" would do?" When I floated the idea to Byron, he seemed less than impressed and flatly told me he would probably not be home before Christmas. Being knocked down again left me feeling sad, mad, frustrated, aggravated, and confused.

The one tiny nugget of hope I got from that brief phone conversation with Byron was he told me I was welcome to visit anytime, and he gave me his new room number. He explained that his health had not been great, and that was the reason he hadn't gotten in touch with me. I took this as an opportunity to head back to the hospital and try one more time to show him how much I "might" like him. I started my mission at Walmart by buying a small tabletop Christmas tree and some red and gold decorations. I picked up a steak burrito, just as I remembered he liked it, and I gathered some courage along the way to make the now-familiar drive to the hospital. As I helped him eat his steak burrito, I shared my love for Christmas and how I believed everyone should be able to enjoy decorations. He wasn't super into it, but we both agreed that Christmas was the best holiday, so he agreed to let me put up a small tree in his hospital room.

A Christmas Miracle

The emotional roller coaster had started again in my heart, and hope seemed to rise. I got to work right away decorating the Christmas tree with lights, tinsel, ornaments, and a star on top. As I plugged it in, Byron's face lit up as bright as the tree itself. He loved it! I stayed for several hours, and we talked about everything. He shared the story of how he came to believe in Jesus and we talked about our Church experiences and what Christmas traditions we had. He introduced each member of his family by name, making it the most enjoyable time we had spent together since our lunch date in June. As I was leaving, Byron asked me to hug

him, and I immediately agreed and literally bounced out of that hospital. The Christmas Tree changed everything!

From that time forward, conversations became more frequent and personal. Our friendship was finally beginning to grow. Phone calls took on a deeper meaning as we began opening up more to each other. He also began healing and got out of the hospital the day before Christmas. He allowed me to pick him up from the hospital and take him home, asking me if I could take the Christmas tree home with us and put it up again at his house. I said, YES!

His trust in me was growing as he gave me his keys and allowed me to pick him up in the van and take him home. With the now-important Christmas tree in tow, I safely transported everyone and everything home. A caregiver was waiting for him at home so our visit was short, but I couldn't help but feel we had taken a big step of trust in our relationship. When I left that night, he had a lit-up, decorated mini-Christmas tree! My heart was full!

Chapter THREE

It Is Well With My Soul

After Christmas, Byron's health seemed to improve every day. His broken leg wasn't causing as much pain or trauma, and he could go back to work. We talked often and had a great time getting to know each other. Sundays were often dedicated to church events or traveling around North Carolina to support disability ministries. I became a great driver, and we had so much fun singing and dancing on our trips to the different churches that he visited for work.

Most of Byron's work was with small group meetings or events for families with disabilities. Typically, I sat back and did whatever he needed. I carried his materials, smiled a lot, and tried to look pretty. A few times, I was able to hear Byron preach. It was incredible, fitting perfectly with everything that I had learned about him. He preached from the Bible, demonstrating his deep connection with God. He was well-spoken and easy to understand. He was funny and engaging, and each time he spoke, there were tears of joy, sadness, or hope. Byron displayed the goodness of God in every sermon I heard him preach.

One night, we traveled to the foothills of NC so that he could preach at a church where a man named Dustin had recently become paralyzed. Byron and Dustin had become friends, and now his small country church wanted to know how they could offer support. This was the first night that I heard Byron tell his story from the pulpit. He had shared his story with me and I knew most of the details, but this night was different. The words that come to mind after hearing his story are heart-wrenching, tear-jerking, powerful, direct, reliance on God, and submission to God's will.

This is what Byron preached that night...

"I was a typical young teenage boy. I liked anything with a ball and anything outside. Baseball, basketball, football, skateboarding, swimming. My brother and I were always

outside, either in the neighborhood, in a pool, or on a ball field. My life was good. My family was good. My parents took us to church on Sunday and Wednesday. I had a great youth group and best friends. On this particular Sunday night, our pastor asked me and 3 other boys to return some tables that we had borrowed from a church nearby. I jumped in the cab of a truck with 3 of my friends and made one of the biggest mistakes of my life. I did not put my seatbelt on. We were on the way and it started to rain. Tracey was driving when we went around a curve and ran off the road. He over-corrected and ran off the other side of the road. The truck started flipping, and Jason went through the windshield and cleared the glass. I followed him out the window at 45 mph, hitting the hood of the truck and bouncing onto the ground.

My life changed in a matter of seconds. With one wrong move, I went from being athletic, popular, and having everything in my life the way I wanted it to be, to being limited, paralyzed, and being completely dependent on everybody for everything. My life dramatically turned upside down. That night, I remember lying on the ground, hearing my friends asking if I was okay, and the sirens. I opened my eyes but couldn't see anything. My friend was standing over me and asked what he could do and told him to turn my head straight. Then the EMTs arrived, and I heard them saying, "That's one of those Sellers boys." I was loaded into the ambulance and taken to the hospital. Once I got to the hospital, I heard my mom crying and the doctors telling her it looked like I would be paralyzed. I spent the next 6 months in the hospital at Chapel Hill, learning how to do almost everything again. I couldn't move from the chest down, so I had to learn how to use braces on my arms to feed myself, brush my teeth, shave, and do almost everything.

I was mad at God and asked why a lot. I couldn't understand how a good God would allow this to happen to me. I was an excellent baseball player and had a great life. I was a good kid and did the right thing. I got good grades

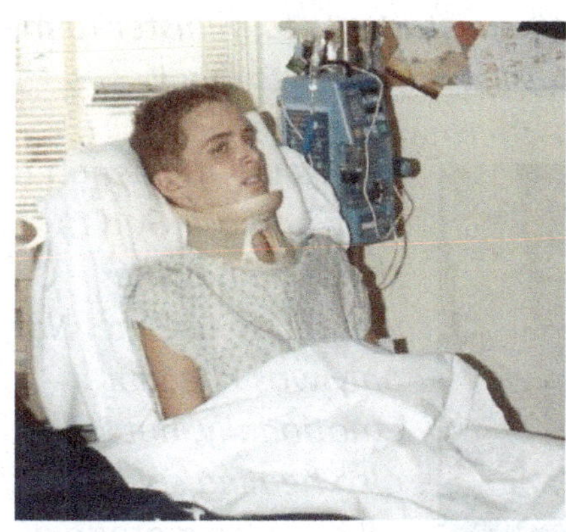

and obeyed my parents. I was running an errand for the church; I didn't deserve this. Being paralyzed did not just change my life, it changed my family's life. My parents had to help me with everything, all the basic daily things. My brother didn't have a friend to play ball and run around with anymore. Everything was different.

I graduated from high school with the help of tutors and my parents. I went to college at St. Andrews in Laurinburg and I had to learn how to find people to help me with the most basic of things. While I was in college, a group of college students who were Christians invited me to do things with them. They invited me to church, dinners, and events. They even invited me to Walmart to hang out. One day we went to Walmart, about 6 of us and we were just hanging out in the toy aisle being obnoxious college kids. I was driving my wheelchair at the end of an aisle and I got hit with a football. My first thought was, WOW this is abuse ... throwing a football at a person who can't walk or even hold a football! Then, I found myself playing dodgeball around Walmart. The goal of the game was to tag me with a football, but I was faster than my friends!

This was the beginning of my emotional healing. I realized that these were my friends and that I could have a life in the chair. I had spent a lot of time shaking my fist at God and asking why or trying to negotiate with God. I even prayed and asked to just heal my hands if He wouldn't heal my legs. God used these college students to minister to me and show me that there was life if I chose to live it.

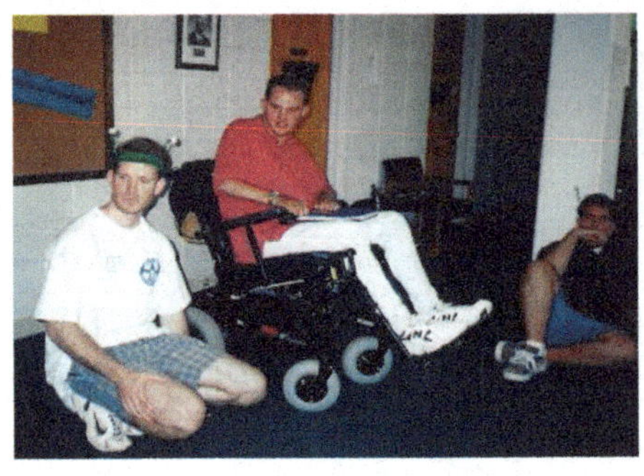

At this point, I began to pray and ask God to show me how he wanted to use me. Not only was I healing emotionally, but I was also healing spiritually. All because a group of people showed me kindness. My story and my life, no matter how you look at it, were not fair from a human perspective. But God took it, and He used it, and he ended up giving me opportunities to reach out and minister to other people in a way that I would have never done if I wasn't in this situation. There are hard days and days I want to give up, but what keeps me going are the promises in His good book. I know God has a purpose and plan for my life and my situation, and I know He will fulfill his promises to never leave me or forsake me. I know He is preparing an eternal home for me in heaven one day."

Byron's message went beyond his testimony as he opened his Bible and shared a passage from Mark 2. As I would come to find out, Byron always connected his story to God's Story. That night, he shared the story of four people who delivered their paralyzed friend to the feet of Jesus. As Byron related his life to the story in the book of Mark, the message to the congregation was clear. Just bring Dustin to Jesus, as often as you can.

I was beginning to realize that God's plan for Byron's life was bigger and deeper than I could imagine. He was happy, content, and extremely confident about God's ability to bring purpose out of his tragedy. His outlook had shifted from hopelessness to hopefulness as he took every opportunity to be used by God. Byron's attitude towards his life was, "It is well with my soul!" What a motto to live by.

Chapter FOUR

Adventures in Real Life

As we continued to get to know each other, I noticed a few things about Byron. He consistently had this "brown leather folder-type thing" on his lap, with his wallet, an all-purpose towel, and his Bible stacked perfectly on top. These seemed to be his standard set-up for the day, and his most precious items. You could often find him outdoors, tilted back in his wheelchair, reading the Bible, and soaking up the sun like a lazy lizard.

Off-Road Adventures

One of Byron's adventures into the outdoors involved driving his fancy blue wheelchair with his necessary "brown thing" items to a nearby park. He found a spot near the pond at the park and, as usual, opened his Bible, read a bit, closed his eyes, and tilted his chair back so his body was almost horizontal to the ground. On this particular day, Byron didn't realize that the ground under his back wheels was damp from rain the day before, and suddenly, he found himself flipped backward. Picture a paralyzed man, arms, and legs unable to move, flipped backward in the mud, and strapped into the wheelchair with a seatbelt. What a beautiful mess!

When I saw Byron that afternoon, he was a dirty mess, with leaves on the back of his shirt and his clothes completely disheveled. Normally, Byron took great care of his appearance, always making sure his clothes were neatly tucked in. However, on this day, Byron's clothes were a complete mess. Excitedly, he recounted the story of his time with Jesus, describing how he ended up on his back while he heard a lady running towards him, shouting, "I'm coming, I'm coming, I work with the physically disabled and mentally retarded, I can help!"

Byron continued his story with a serious look on his face, "It is 2018 and those are not words that anyone should use these days, but since I was upside down on the ground, I decided to let her help. I guess I fit into 1 or both categories." Byron finished the story with a straight face and said, "Thank God that he put a lady at the park who wasn't afraid of an upside-down quadriplegic laying in the grass." He was not upset by any of these happenings. To him, it was an off-road adventure that became another one of his well-told stories. I was laughing hysterically as I imagined the scene at the park and He began laughing at himself as he finished with, "I also have to say thank God that she was Superman and could flip me over like a pancake and get me back in my chair!"

Independent Adventures

As Byron and I got to know each other, we had many conversations about his accident and the events that followed. One of my favorite stories about Byron's healing was how his family cared for him while he was still in high school. As a typical high school student, Byron was

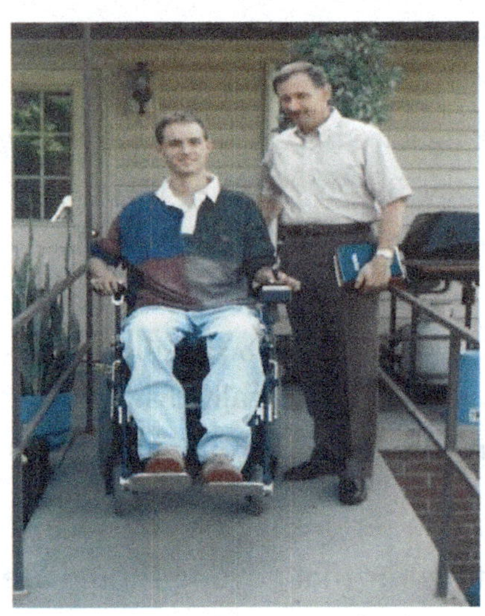

concerned about his appearance and going into public in his chair. One day, Byron's dad told him to get ready because they were going out. Although Byron was less than eager, his dad, Mr. Don, made him get in the van and they headed off to the mall. They walked and rolled throughout the mall, talking to people, window shopping, and hanging out in public like normal people. As Byron told the story many years later, he still had some hard feelings, but was full of gratitude for his dad. He recognized and often told others that his dad was vital in his recovery. Mr. Don did not allow Byron to stay home and feel sorry for himself.

The loving push from Byron's parents helped him become independent, graduate from 2 colleges, move to Charlotte, and secure a full-time job. I realized after an afternoon spent with his parents that I had a lot to learn about continuing this loving push in Byron's life. One afternoon, his parents were spending time with Byron and me at his condo. Byron asked me to get a mint for him. As I had done many times, I got a mint and put it in his mouth. His dad focused directly on me and said, "Don't do that again. He can pick up his own mint." Put it on his brown thing and make him get it in his mouth." I quickly responded, "Yes sir, of course!" From that moment on, I got what he needed and put it on his lap. He had to use his strength to get what he wanted to his mouth! What an amazing father he was to encourage independence and freedom in his son.

Being around his parents, I learned a little more about Byron's background. After high school, Byron went to St. Andrews College because they had a dorm for students with disabilities that provided caregivers and nurses. This made the transition from home to college a little easier as he continued to discover how to do life in a chair. Being in the chair was not always sunshine and rainbows for Byron, especially on a college campus. He told me a story of driving his chair to a lake on St Andrew's campus and asking God for a miracle. Byron prayed and cried out to the Lord, saying, "if you just heal my hands I will serve you." He reasoned with God, believing that since he had surrendered his life at an early age and since the accident was connected to an errand for the church, surely God would do this for him. At this point in Byron's life, he didn't know that God was healing his heart, not his hands.

Byron's life began to change as a group of students befriended him and treated him like any other student. He realized God could use him just the way he was and discovered a new passion for living and a brighter outlook on the future. After 2 years in the dorm, Byron transitioned to finding his own caregivers and became even more independent. Byron graduated confident that he could not only achieve his academic goals but also navigate his newfound freedom with success.

Byron then transferred to Columbia International University, where college life was very different. The absence of nurses or dorms for physically disabled students posed a challenge for Byron. Byron's refusal to give up (he never knew the word "quit") motivated him to work with the university and renovate a dorm room that catered to his specific needs. This allowed him to attend graduate school and experience campus life alongside his peers. He earned a degree in Bible and a Master's degree in counseling. Joni and Friends, an international disability ministry, recruited him to be a part of their team in the Charlotte, North Carolina area. Byron moved to Charlotte and once again had to find accessible housing.

Initially, Byron's best option for housing was in an assisted living facility. Byron was the youngest person in the home by at least 30 years! Being the clown that he was, Byron would often arrive after work while the residents were playing BINGO in the gathering hall. He had developed relationships with many of the residents and they all knew him as a fast-moving

young man. What they soon learned about Byron was his sense of humor and mischievous ways. One night, while everyone was playing a serious game of BINGO, Byron rode through the hall yelling "B-57, G-2, O-89! Many of the residents were genuinely confused because Byron's bingo numbers didn't match the numbers on their cards. After a few of Byron's antics, the residents caught on and began throwing BINGO chips at him. Somehow, Byron could always bring laughter and joy to the simplest of events.

Eventually, Byron saved enough money and began the quest to find a proper home. It would need to be totally accessible, and he had all the details worked out in his head. His home would need a flat entrance with no stairs, a large master bedroom with a roll-in shower, lowered countertops, sinks, and light switches. The smallest details were huge, and he had to think through things I had never thought about. The location would need to be just right for any future caregivers to access the bus line in case they didn't have transportation. With all these specifications in mind, and using his exceptional collaboration skills, Byron found a builder that could expertly design a brand-new, fully accessible condominium! In 2001, Byron achieved another monumental goal, he became a first-time homeowner.

As my life was merging with Byron's and I was learning more and more about his day-to-day life. I was amazed at his ability to walk through challenging situations with joy in his heart and a smile on his face. I could only conclude that this ability came from his REAL relationship and TOTAL dependency on Jesus Christ.

Dating Adventures

By February 2003, Byron and I had spent quite a lot of time together. Our friendship was growing and our lives were working together nicely. I was learning as much about him and his life as he was about me. Valentine's Day was coming, and I felt nervous about our relationship. Byron was old-school and didn't believe in casual dating. His belief was that if a man and woman are dating, they should be prepared to marry each other. This differed greatly from my ideas of dating, and I wasn't even sure if he was interested in me. It seemed like we both only had one serious relationship in the past, and I thought the point of dating was to decide if you love someone enough to marry them. Byron didn't agree. And then there was the unspoken presence of all Byron's women friends. While getting to know Byron, I noticed that a lot of his friends were women. The mystery lady in the chair at the hospital that I met on an earlier visit, the lady who leaves food every week. All of them were his friends. Some would take him to work, or doctors' appointments, or just come to visit. Women were a constant presence in Byron's life. Was I just another woman who was helping him? Did he think of me as any different from how he thought of all the other women? I wasn't sure of my place in Byron's world, but I knew that since the Christmas Tree experience; we were closer, and I was interested in being more than a friend to him.

Three days before Valentine's Day, Byron asked if I wanted to go out for Valentine's Dinner on the day after Valentine's Day. His best friend Anthony and his girlfriend would join us and I was excited because this seemed like it might be the first official date since June. We made a plan, and it seemed like things were moving in the right direction. At least from my perspective.

Valentine's Dinner was anything but typical. When we got to the crowded restaurant, they did not prepare me for our party being the center of attention. Everyone was staring at us and in my typical fashion, I was beat red and didn't know what to do. When they showed us to our table, Byron couldn't get his chair to the table. Can you imagine the stares from all the people trying to enjoy their meals? As the server and I were red-faced and trying to deal with our embarrassment issues, I noticed that Bryon and Anthony were cracking jokes and laughing. This did not bother them at all. Just when I thought I couldn't be more mortified, a couple that was nearby decided to stand up and offer us their table. Since they had already been served, this required an additional commotion, as everything on their table had to be moved over to ours. I could have melted on the floor. Once we got settled at our new table, Byron turned to me and said, "Welcome to my world." Again, he and Anthony busted out laughing! I was speechless. Dinner was filled with lots of laughter and happiness between Byron and his friends. They were incredibly kind and accepting of me, and I felt myself gradually recovering from the earlier seating debacle.

Later that night, we went to a hockey game and then back to Byron's condo. As we were chatting and talking about life and all the fun we had that night, Byron finally asked the question I was waiting to hear! "Would you want to be my girlfriend?" he asked, followed by a long explanation of his ideas on dating. We discussed our intentions and hopes for our relationship and even though I didn't completely agree that dating should be solely with the intent of marriage, I wasn't opposed, either. So by the end of the night, I was Byron Seller's girlfriend! Friday, February 15th, 2003, was the beginning of my new life with an amazing man!

Chapter FIVE

Lessons from Byron

Lessons on God

We went bowling. Did you know you can bowl without using your hands? We went roller skating. Did you know you could roller skate without using your feet? Sometimes we got dressed up fancy and went to shows and restaurants downtown. Other times, we hung out in regular clothes and just stayed in the backyard or walked around the neighborhood. He loved sunrises, sunsets, the beach, and any body of water. He tolerated my happy place, the mountains. We talked a lot; prayed together; read our Bibles together; and asked questions of each other. We seemed to make each other better.

What stood out to me the most at this point in our relationship was Byron's relationship with God. He not only had a personal relationship with God, but he depended on Him. Byron depended on God to speak to him, guide him, give him wisdom, provide people to help with his daily needs, and much more. It went beyond being a mere topic of conversation for him; it was a daily practice. As a country girl who grew up in a small Baptist church, I knew about God and had asked Him to be my Savior. I believed that I had a meaningful relationship with God and that it was going well. But it amazed me as Byron showed me, in his humble way, that I needed to do more to develop my relationship with Jesus Christ. He did this without even realizing how he was affecting my life.

Lessons on Dependency

Time with Byron was always an adventure. What I was learning was just how dependent Byron was. He depended on caregivers to show up every morning and every night to help him with his basic needs. I noticed good caregivers were difficult to find, and when you open the doors of your home and invite people in to assist you, you never know what's going to happen. I quickly learned that Byron was extraordinarily patient.

As I became more comfortable and closer with Byron, I was impatient and judgmental about the quality of his care. Byron often reminded me he needed this support system and that it was his responsibility to make the best of it. As I pondered his position on this matter and what our life together might look like, I realized Byron was content with his life. Sometimes Byron would reflect on how different his life would have been without the accident. His life at college, playing baseball, and all the other things that he had dreamed of doing. Nevertheless, after many years, Byron was convinced that this was God's deliberate plan for him and it was good. Not only did he live a life dependent on other people, but he also lived a life dependent on God.

That dependency came creeping back on a cold and rainy Thursday night when we had plans to go to dinner and a speaking engagement for Byron's work. All the details were in place, but when we got to his van, the lift wouldn't work. We made many attempts to fix it, call others to fix it, or find another vehicle to put him in. But in the end, the well-made plans would have to change. Nonchalantly, Byron began letting people know he could not attend. I kept trying to come up with solutions going on about ideas to fix the problem. Byron turned to me and calmly said, "Scarlet, if you are going to do this life with me, you're going to have to learn to deal with disappointment."

"What??" I was hysterical. We had plans, he had work, and something needed to be done. How could he be calm and peaceful about the van not working? How could this be the way things turned out? I was still thinking, maybe I can call my dad, he can fix anything! Byron quickly stopped me and reminded me it was okay. Although Byron got frustrated and upset at times, it was never over things that he couldn't control. He believed things happened for a reason. A year had passed since he was hospitalized for tubing down a river and breaking his femur. He was accustomed to disruption in his life, and yet Byron was at peace. He was living his life dependent on Christ and was content and happy to be healthy and serving the Lord. Could I learn from that? Absolutely! That single night of disappointment was over and life went on. We rescheduled dinner, got the van fixed, and just as Byron reminded me, everything worked out fine.

Lessons on Fun, Friendship, and Food

Byron never turned down an opportunity to have fun. Being with people and trying new things was fun for him. He had a genuine love for people from different cultures and enjoyed eating dinner with the family across the street from Ethiopia or hanging out at an Indian friend's house, hoping to sample a traditional meal. You could find him with friends at the local Mexican restaurant or listening to a friend's problem over a cup of coffee at Starbucks. No matter where he was or what he was eating, he found people to talk to and build a relationship with.

Anyone who knew Byron knew he ate like a 12-year-old boy. The doctors told Byron he had diabetes, but that didn't stop him. Many people who knew him didn't even know he was a diabetic and multiple women in his workplace kept candy stashes just for Byron. Each of them was unaware that others provided him a "sweet treat" throughout the day. He was a meat and potatoes kind of guy with cheese on everything! Good conversation and good food were often the highlight of his day, and he frequently expressed that the people he ate with were the true source of greatness, not the food.

Byron frequently had to go to Atlanta, Georgia for appointments with doctors, specialists, or to repair his van. Once again, Bryon depended on a ride to and from. This would require a long day of driving and waiting, and often Byron's friend Gerry would be his chauffeur for the day. Gerry's nickname was "Pop" and he loved to eat as much as Byron did. One day, hunger struck, but it wasn't time for a meal yet. They stopped to get food and came up with the phrase "appetite suppressant." I wondered why they didn't just call it a snack or a meal, and Byron quickly explained that an "appetite suppressant" was bigger than a snack but smaller than a meal. He also clarified that it didn't mean that a meal wouldn't be necessary in a few hours! "Appetite suppressants" became a regular part of Byron's travel requirements!

Lessons From the Pier

Byron loved the beach. His parents have many stories of his beach trips with family and friends as he was growing up. Playing in the sand and ocean was one of his favorite places to go on trips. After being paralyzed, getting on the beach was harder and required more planning. He didn't let that stop him. He enjoyed getting in a beach wheelchair and hanging out on the sand. When he couldn't get on the sand, he found peace on the pier. Byron would spend hours at the end of the pier, watching the water and listening to the waves crash. Of course, He would take all his important items, especially his Bible. He would tilt back, relax, and soak up the beach atmosphere while spending time with God. He often said that his best conversations with the Lord happened on the pier. He purposefully met people on the pier and talked to them about life and Jesus. Of course, after we had children, I believed he was on the pier watching us play in the ocean, but he was also growing his relationship with God as he sat and enjoyed the salty air and endless sights and sounds of the beach!

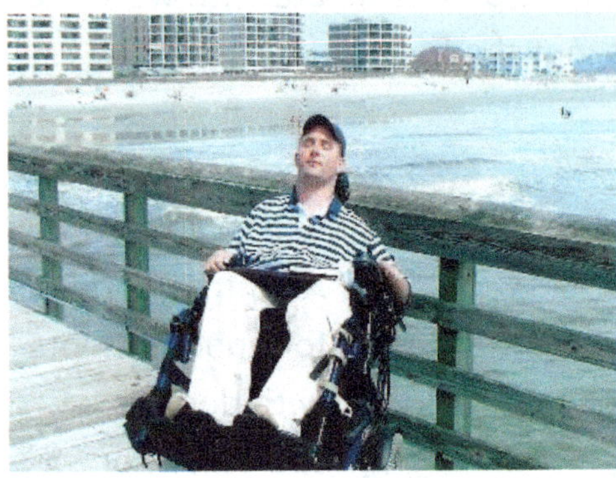

Lessons for the Future

On the important topic of food, Fuddruckers was one of Byron's favorite places to eat. Thankfully, he loved eating out with me, so he took me to his favorite restaurants. Byron and I had gotten to know each other pretty well, and we were comfortable sharing different parts of our lives. As we pulled into the parking space, I noticed the parking lot wasn't very full. Before lowering the van ramp, Byron made eye contact with me and asked in his most serious voice, "Do you feel ready to help me relieve myself?"

WHAT?? Relieve yourself? What did he mean? I was scrambling for the words to ask, are you serious? We were in a restaurant parking lot with no bathroom nearby. He insisted on explaining in great detail that he had already relieved himself and just needed assistance to dispose of it properly. I burst out laughing and quickly replied, "You're joking, right!"

He was not joking around. By this time, He was laughing and giving me an out, as he did so well. He was known for asking people to help with something and then talking them out of it. So, he began talking me out of something that I had not agreed to do and didn't know how to do. As he lowered the lift and fully exited the van, Byron explained that if I wanted to help with the most basic tasks or watering the plants, he could walk me through it. Reluctantly, I stood at a curb with his feet over the shrubs as he explained to me what to touch, what to flip, and where to put my feet! After about 2 minutes, he began backing his chair away from the curb and said, "Thanks for helping me water the plants. They are no longer thirsty!" And off we went into the restaurant for dinner! Fortunately, there was an indoor restroom where I could wash my hands, collect my thoughts, and ponder, "Will life always be like this?""

Lessons on Laughter

Another thing I was learning about Bryon was what a jokester he was. One of my favorite stories to hear him tell was about his blooming friendship with Anthony,

nicknamed Birdsong. Anthony was a graduate student at CIU, and a big cut-up. He was loud and fun and became one of Byron's best friends. They often referred to themselves as brothers from different mothers. One story about these two brothers happened while Byron was studying in his dorm room at college. Byron would often need to cross his legs occasionally to relieve pressure points during long days of studying. On this day, he had gotten someone to cross one of his feet over the other before Anthony arrived. Anthony walked into Byron's room and immediately started talking. Suddenly, he stopped and asked Byron, "How did you cross your legs?" Byron looked to the left and looked to the right as if he was making sure no one else was around. He whispered, “I’m not paralyzed. I’m here with the CIA! Don’t tell anyone! Shhhh!!!” Anthony’s eyes got as big as saucers and he whispered back, “Really? Why are you at a Christian college?” Byron burst out laughing and said, “No Birdsong, I’m truly PARALYZED! My friend Tim crossed my legs early today and I really can’t move them!” I’m sure the angels in heaven could hear Birdsong and Byron laughing! He was never too serious and always looked for a way to make people laugh.

Lessons on Love

Over the months of our dating life, I witnessed Byron do many things that I assumed a paralyzed person could never do. He always seemed to find a way to accomplish the things he wanted to do. I witnessed a real joy that came from a genuine relationship with God. A dependency created by a tragic accident that he used to build relationships, love people, and achieve his goals. With a childlike spirit, a passionate heart, and a sky's the limit mentality, he lived life to the fullest.

Byron asked to take me to dinner at a fancy restaurant in Charlotte. He told me that his favorite outfit was a blue flowered skirt I had, and he asked me to wear it on our date. Naturally, if he thought I was cute in that skirt, I would have it on! I got to his house, and he was wearing a suit. He looked smokin' hot! He directed me to drive to our usual parking lot downtown, but as I headed towards one of our regular spots, I realized he had other intentions. He went up to a fancy building that I had never seen before and reached the door before me in order to open it. (Thank God for electric doors!) He was quite the gentleman! We got into the elevator and went to the top floor. When the door opened, a man dressed in a tuxedo welcomed us and said in a very serious voice, "Mr. Sellers, right this way."

I was so confused. What is happening right now? Who was this man and how did he know Byron? We entered a huge room with windows all around, tables with white tablecloths and lots of silverware and candles. The only people I saw were dressed in tuxedos and holding trays. The serious man from the elevator guided us to a table in a corner, with a beautiful view of planes coming and going from the nearby airport. There were rose petals on the tables and it looked like something out of a movie. As I did often, I began asking questions. Byron was not interested in my questions and told me to sit and enjoy the view and that he would be right back. Seriously... he just left me there...alone. I felt really anxious because it was the fanciest place I had ever been, and Byron had set it up so that we had the entire restaurant to ourselves! A few minutes later, he appeared with a ring box on his lap. It hit me at that moment that he had a much bigger question on his mind than the girlfriend question he had asked back a few months ago! As he got to our table, I started to cry. To this day, I have no idea what he said but I'm sure it was sweet. I do remember him asking, "Will you marry me? I had no doubt in my mind that being a permanent part of this man's life would make me a better person!

Chapter SIX

The Run-Over Bride

I said yes! Wedding planning began and building our life together was moving forward. Byron was not a traditional groom, so our wedding would be nothing short of non-traditional.

I was blissfully in love with this amazing man and yet I realized some of my friends didn't agree with my choice. They felt I was settling for someone who couldn't provide for me or do the things I enjoyed. Somehow, they were afraid of his curved fingers, or that he would spend the rest of his life in a wheelchair. I was confused by their refusal to see past his lifeless legs to notice a heart that was full of wisdom and love for me. As friends disappeared and things changed, I realized that this was what life with Byron would be like. Some people would understand our life and be happy for us, and some would not.

Our engagement period was full of confirmation of the Lord's blessing and His will for our lives. Byron's kindness and grace rubbed off on me and He helped me continue to reach out a hand of friendship to those who rejected us. He helped me discover a new way of fixing problems by giving them to God. Together; we prayed for healing, support, and encouragement as we prepared to be married.

Our wedding planner, Karen, was a special lady who had spent the previous 4 years pouring into Byron's life. She was his weekly chauffeur, driving 25 minutes across town to help him get where he needed to go. Byron described Karen as an angel that God sent to help him navigate Charlotte. She delivered a meal each week from a "mystery lady" who wanted to bless him with home-cooked meals. Byron had no idea who this mystery lady was, but her cooking and generosity blessed him. The conversation and friendship between him and his angel Karen deepened as she selflessly provided for him each week.

As we planned our wedding at a local church, some logistics needed to be worked out. Steps led up to the

pulpit area, so a friend added a ramp as a personal touch for our service. It was important to Byron and me to sit eye-to-eye during our vows. So, we decided I would sit in a beautiful chair that was the perfect height as we held hands, shared rings, and committed our lives to each other. Byron's childhood pastor married us because we wanted to honor the deep connection he had with Byron. We designed the service to be personal, point people to Jesus, and show our unconditional love for each other. We chose people who were special to us to sing, play piano, decorate, or set food out in the reception hall. Our ceremony genuinely blessed us, as it reflected over 20 years of friendships and relationships.

Our wedding day was a picture of what I believe heaven will look like. Besides our own families, there were people of diverse generations, ethnic groups, levels of rich and poor, and those whose bodies were able and disabled. For us, this gathering was a picture of the love God created when He wove our lives together. It represented a huge circle of diversity that would forever be a reflection of Him. We were not alone in embarking on this journey of marriage, but love surrounded us from many places in our life and the world. While sitting in front of God and our village, we laughed, we cried, we prayed, and we dreamed of the future.

After I got to kiss my husband for the first time, we headed down the ramp together! I breathed a sigh of relief as he got off the stage without running off the ramp or over anyone. As I skipped alongside Byron down the aisle, I felt a tug on my long and strapless wedding dress. As I continued out the door of the sanctuary, I glanced down. Suddenly, Byron's chair stopped abruptly, jolting me.

As I looked down, his black tire had turned to white and my dress was completely wrapped around the wheel! Instantaneously, my sister came running behind us yelling,

"Byron, stop! You can't take her dress off yet!" Everyone was laughing. I was mortified. Yet, somehow, the tire marks left behind on the beautiful wedding dress were a perfect picture of the imperfect life that lay ahead of us.

Chapter SEVEN

All in the Family Life

And so it began! We were finally a family. I moved into his little 2-bedroom condo and the adventures continued from our dating days. Caregivers came and went in the morning and evenings, always bringing with them a laugh or cry! Byron continued in ministry with Joni and Friends, and I was teaching in the local school system. If we weren't at a sporting event, we spent our weekends traveling to places like The Biltmore, the beach, the mountains, or to visit his family.

Man on a Mission

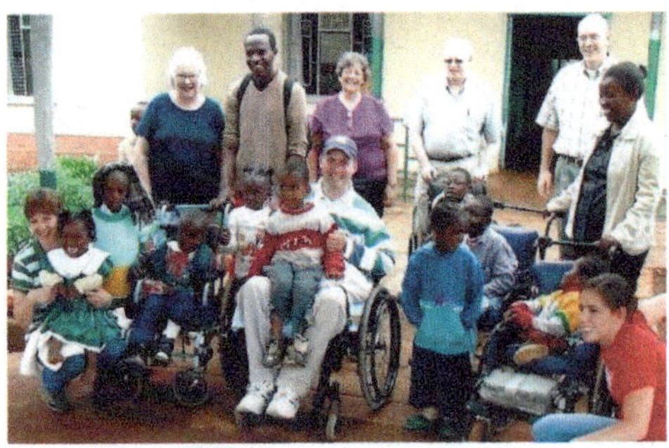

Byron took on a project with Joni and Friends and a local church to deliver wheelchairs to Nairobi, Kenya. For months, he planned the trip, gathered funds, and organized a team of therapists and volunteers. We packed 200 wheelchairs in a shipping container and sent them off to Africa. Byron handled logistics for hotels, meals, transportation, and giveaway sites throughout the Nairobi region. He assembled a 14-person team from all over the United

States, most of whom had never been on an international mission trip before! God blessed us and provided all the financial support we needed to go on the trip together. Byron was eager to bring mobility and Jesus to Kenya.

Byron had developed friendships with some pastors at Nairobi Baptist Church who asked him to preach on the Sunday we were there. He took this opportunity seriously and spent lots of time praying about how and what to share from God's Word. The church was a large international church that drew many people from the surrounding cities.

Wheelchair access was nonexistent in Nairobi, so Byron had to find ways to get around since he could not transfer out of his wheelchair and into a van or car. The church had steps, making it impossible for Byron to reach the stage, so the church men built a ramp so he could roll right up to the pulpit on Sunday morning. It was a great example of God's love for the church.

On the Sunday Byron was to preach, the church invited people with disabilities from all over the area. They embraced the ideas in Luke 14:4 about how loving people considered to be "the least of these" is equal to loving Jesus. While we were there, we visited an orphanage and

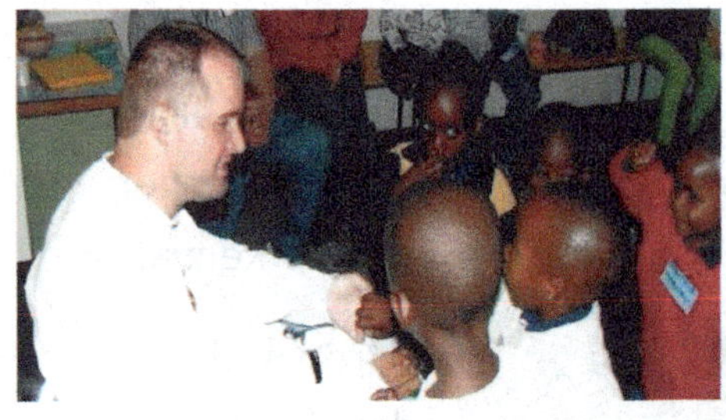

spent time with young children who were abandoned by their biological parents. Getting to hold them, feed them, play games with them, and show them the love of Jesus was an incredible blessing. Our visit to Nairobi was an experience that changed our lives forever.

We loved it so much that we returned a few years later, with the desire to minister to families with disabilities in more remote areas of Kenya. We met with people in their homes, prayed with them, encouraged them, and pointed them to Jesus. Byron continued to have discussions with the local pastors about the importance of including individuals with disabilities in the Kingdom of God.

Family Life

Byron and I began talking about having children and expanding our family. I distinctly remember Byron calling one morning on my way to work, asking me to pray specifically that the Lord would provide an accessible home with many rooms that we could fill with children. Byron and I had discussed having children while we were dating, but not seriously. Our experience at the orphanage in Kenya left a big impression on us about the importance of adoption. So we began to research what that might look like for us.

As we explored all the options for adoption, we quickly realized that adopting internationally was probably not something that was a reality for us because of the regulations that international countries have in place for adoption. So, we began filling out forms and completing all the required tasks to be approved for a domestic adoption.

As our life was changing and growing, God answered our prayer for a house that might meet our needs. Once again, Byron played an integral part in designing it so that it would meet all of his needs. Plans called for lowering the light switches, widening the door frames, and installing the cabinets at just the right height. Byron especially loved the roll-in shower in his bathroom, which became his favorite part of the house. While our home was being built, we wrote Bible verses on the framework and asked God to fill it with laughter, love, and joy.

While in this building process, we also found ourselves conflicted about how to fill out the adoption forms. We were required to answer questions and check boxes about a child's race, or special needs that we are okay with. The form gave options like a child with a cleft palate, cerebral palsy, or a child born addicted to drugs. Byron was careful and thoughtful in his decision-making process. We prayed and sought guidance from God to help us answer these questions. We wondered how we could put a check beside some characteristics and not others and how these selections would affect God's will for our family.

One afternoon, Byron went to spend time with the Lord at his favorite spot in our neighborhood. He rolled over to a small "bunny trail" where he would often sit and watch families as they walked by. He came home that day, after his time with the Lord, and excitedly said, 'We can fill out those forms tonight!' I seemed a bit confused about exactly what forms he was talking about, so he clarified he was ready to complete and submit the adoption forms! Byron explained that a man and woman walked by while he was praying and the Lord spoke to him, saying, ‘that is what your family will look like.' The couple was walking a yellow lab, a black mixed breed, and a gray Great Dane. Byron was 100% convinced that the Lord was telling him that our family would look like a picture of heaven. We would have children of different races and a variety of needs. We completed the adoption forms that night, checking all the different races and disabilities, and left the other details up to the Lord.

Fast forward several years, God created our adoption story with a biracial baby, an African American baby, and a 14-year-old "brown" boy from Vietnam. We filled all the rooms in our home with children, and Byron and I believe God revealed his perfect plan through the neighborhood dogs on their nightly walk.

Byron and I deeply believed that allowing our children to know their biological parents; and the blessing we received when God chose us to be their parents was vital to their emotional well-being. So, we had semi-open adoptions with each of the families because we wanted to show love

to the parents who had made such a hard decision. As we met with each set of parents, we promised them we would love their child endlessly. In only the way Byron could, he connected with two 16-year-olds who were not in a relationship and had no interest in being parents. He somehow found common ground with a 32-year-old African American woman with 4 other children and promised her we would protect her child, make happy memories, and point her to Jesus. Later, Byron took on the role of a father figure to a troubled 14-year-old Vietnamese boy with a struggling family. He found himself immersed in soccer games, middle school homework, and an immense love for the last puzzle piece in this mosaic family. Byron's example of living his life for Christ touched the lives of not only our children, but their biological families as well.

Byron was an amazing girl-Dad! He took them for rides in his wheelchair, sometimes on the back, or on his lap, or on his feet. He was always challenging them to some sort of race. Whether by bike, skates, or scooters, he made sure they knew he was faster in his wheelchair than they were. Byron and Josie enjoyed strolling through the neighborhood, learning all the dog's names, and finding out where everyone lived. He was a great listener and always had patience for her girl drama. As Josie began to grow and found her voice, she became Byron's right hand. She loved going places with him, and he would always allow her to be his helper.

Byron made the best of the time he had one-on-one with each of the kids. Our youngest daughter, Janie, loved it when Byron read stories in funny voices and changed the words to make the girls laugh. Wherever they were, he was engaged. If our girls were on the trampoline, he sat and watched. When they played basketball, he would make them dribble around him as he became the sports commentator. When they played with Barbies or dolls, he played with them. He was an involved dad, just like any other dad, who could crawl on the floor or play sports with their children.

One big milestone for our family came when Byron decided he was going to learn to drive. He purchased a modified van, took a driver training class to learn to use hand controls, and came home one day with a license to drive without relying on others! No one ever thought that would be possible, and it became one of Byron's proudest moments. Driving opened a whole new world for our family. He was no longer dependent on others for transportation and immediately began driving to appointments, family events, and outings with the kids.

Balancing Work and Health

During this time of raising children, Byron transitioned from working at Joni and Friends to working at Steele Creek Church of Charlotte. He began working as a pastor for families with special needs and eventually became the Children's pastor. Byron worked tirelessly and prayed fervently for the special needs and children's ministry at our church. He led by example, and taught our children that church was a place where you found family, peace, and rest, although he did not rest very often. As with most things, work was a bit more complicated for Byron. He had to use an arm brace for writing and a special "bent" fork for eating. He had to constantly think about the difficulties of regulating his diabetes, and most famously, he always needed sugar, coffee, and candy. Byron believed this was an opportunity for him to use his skills to serve the Lord, teach young kids about God, and build relationships with their families. He took a hands-on approach to teaching Bible lessons and always left the kids curious about their faith. Byron's interactions with people pointed back to Christ's love. He had a true and consistent desire for a real relationship with others that mirrored his relationship with Jesus.

As life got busier, Byron struggled with pressure sores from sitting in a wheelchair for more hours than he should have. He was committed to embracing life to its fullest and felt that staying in bed was not truly living. It was rare for him to complain about not feeling well or having frequent doctor appointments. He occasionally spent a day or two in the hospital for pressure sore healing, blood, or fluid treatments, kidney stent insertions, or minor medical help. He faced these challenges without hesitation and continued to live his independent life at full speed.
But in 2016, they diagnosed Byron with an infection in his pelvic and hip bones. He had a pressure sore that had been lingering for almost two years and had exposed part of a bone to the air. The doctors told Byron and me that because of the bone infection; he needed to live in an assisted living center so he could receive around-the-clock nursing care. At that point, we had a four-year-old, a 16-year-old, that had only been with us for two years, and an 8-year-old. I absolutely had to bring their dad home. So, Byron and I decided we would go home, pray, and live life the best we could. We went home on IV antibiotics, did a lot of praying and relying on the Lord, and I became a "nurse" after years of saying, "I am not a nurse, I am his wife."

We developed a new lifestyle of administering IVs, sorting pills, and cooking in healthy ways that were good for all of us. After a few months of focusing on health, medicine, and Byron being out of his chair more than in his chair, he could begin sitting up again. Through God's grace and provision, Byron slowly started living his life again, working again, and making memories with the family.

Love, Laughter, Joy

Dinnertime was fun at our house. Byron had a running joke. He would request more cheese if my cooking wasn't up to par. He believed anything was edible if covered in enough cheese. His parents even told a story about when Byron and his brother were young, and they got a new refrigerator. After the old fridge was taken away, a giant stack of cheese wrappers remained behind the refrigerator! Apparently, Byron was the culprit, as each time he got a piece of cheese, he would throw the wrapper behind the fridge hoping no one would notice!

Byron loved food, and he always knew what he wanted for dinner. We ate at the dinner table and took that opportunity to connect with the kids about their day.

We discussed the highs and lows, things we could or couldn't change, and, of course, sprinkled in some cheesy jokes for added flavor. Byron hated all veggies but would try to get Josie to eat her vegetables by saying, "If I have to eat them, you have to eat with me. I'll take a bite and you take a bite at the same time." I felt like I had hit the lottery because my husband and kids were eating veggies!

After dinner, the girls loved to perform. Byron would play the role of the announcer. He had a great voice to "announce" the girls as they danced through the living

room or put on a fashion show. Most days before bedtime, Bryon talked with the kids about the Lord, emphasizing the importance of dedicating their hearts to Christ. We tried to read the Bible or learn about something in God's Word that applied to our current situation. Before each kid prayed, Byron always said, "Pray like you're praying to the God who created the universe." The kids knew this meant talking to God was serious. Eventually, Byron took part in the baptism of all three of our kids as they made professions of faith in front of our family, friends, and the Lord.

I will always remember his way of saying goodnight to the kids as his caregiver arrived every evening to put him in bed. He made a special point to hug them, kiss them on the head, and tell them goodnight and sweet dreams. Because Byron had limited strength in his arms, he made sure the kids gave an intentional hug and if they didn't, he would say, "Squeeze till it grunts!" The best goodnight hugs came from the side as Byron would lay his head against their head in a special embrace.

Chapter EIGHT

Where the Rubber Meets the Road

Byron spent two hours in the morning and two hours at night with a caregiver. During this time, he made sure that his medical and personal needs were taken care of by a caregiver. It was essential for our marriage, relieving me from the role of nurse or caregiver for most days. Byron had built a special relationship with one of our caregivers, and he made sure that when we traveled, we had saved enough money to bring a caregiver with us. This was an enormous sacrifice, but a way for Byron to honor our vows to be husband and wife. It was a gift to me that Byron took seriously.

As the years went on, Byron continued to smile every day and limit his complaining. No one outside of our home would ever know how much pain he had, his medical complications, or his frustration with doctors, medicines, insurance, and medical supplies. These things took a lot of Byron's time, but he never complained about it. He was a master at planning and making sure everything was scheduled and in order.

The Pandemic

In 2020, when COVID-19 became a pandemic, Bryon continued to put the needs of our kids first. Luoc had gone to college, but the girls were in public school. Byron didn't feel online learning worked for the girls because the screen gave Janie migraines and it constantly distracted Josie. We agreed to begin homeschooling the girls, and he took the very important lead role. During the days, Byron helped with their school assignments while I worked remotely for the school system. This was a great time of connection and learning for Byron and the kids. The beauty of the world shutting down for COVID was that we had more time together as a family. We spent much more time at home making memories, laughing, loving, and learning together.

It was undoubtedly challenging as we were constantly at home, with Byron developing a virtual children's ministry for church families and me adapting to teaching virtually. All of this happened in a small house that had no hiding places. Everyone found it difficult, not just us, but Byron always found the positive in the situation.

"My Body is Tired"

During the same year, Byron personally told me he believed his time on earth was limited. This was the first time I ever heard him say that. Of course, I dismissed what he said and quickly told him that there was no way God would take him and leave me to parent alone. From that point forward, Byron and I had several talks about his feeling that God was going to take him to heaven soon. I knew I was not cut out to be a single parent and besides; I needed him. No matter what I said, Byron stood firm about his time being short.

In May 2020, Janie gave her life to Christ and Byron arranged a time at the church for her to be baptized. It was a sweet time in our family as we gathered from around the state to celebrate Janie's decision. A few months later, Byron mentioned again that he was convinced that his work on earth was drawing to an end. He was not sick; he did not have COVID, and medically, there was no reason for him to feel this way.

Byron was completely honest in our conversations, saying he was tired, not simply tired, but his body was tired. I knew in my heart that Byron had a special relationship with God and that he was consistently right in what he said about his special time with the Lord. But this time, I was unwilling to hear and believe what he was saying. I couldn't imagine life without my best friend, husband, father to our kids, decision-maker, sense of reason, and confidant. Who would help me manage our money and keep everything organized?

On May 19th, 2021, Byron had taken the girls to work with him that morning, as he often did, so they could be his hands on many ministry-related tasks. I had virtual

appointments that day and before noon, Byron called and said he didn't feel well. He was feeling cold and asked me to put his favorite blanket in the dryer so it would be warm when he got home. The complication of Byron being paralyzed included his temperature gauge also being paralyzed. By the time Byron realized he was cold, he felt it deep in his bones, and by the time he realized he was hot, he felt overheated. When he didn't feel good, he put this special blanket I had brought back from a mission trip on his head and wrapped it around his neck. We called it his Mother Mary blanket and when he had it on; we knew he was cold. So, on this day, I thought little of it because often he didn't feel good so he would ask for his blanket. After being home for about an hour, attempting all the usual pain relief methods, and observing his sweaty and clammy condition (another sign of an issue), I began to get worried. Typically, one of the three P's (Pain, Pee, or Poop) caused his problems. I noticed him on the back patio, sitting in the sun with the blanket wrapped around his head. I could hear him talking to someone from the church, but he was weak and having difficulty breathing. Like most men, Byron hated going to the doctor and always wanted to wait it out. Finally, several hours later, I convinced him to go to the ER.

As we left, he hugged the kids and told them he would be back soon. He told them he didn't feel well and needed to figure out what was wrong. He mentioned he probably just needed some fluids and medicine and assured them he would be back soon. When we arrived at the ER, they immediately took him to a room and people began poking, prodding, and running tests. I wasn't expecting that kind of reception, and things seemed to get worse. Byron was sweating and struggling to take a deep breath. He was quiet and didn't seem to be responding to the fluids. Knowing how much Byron and I loved sports and would often have battles about who was better, Lebron James or Steph Curry, I turned on the Lakers and Golden State game, hoping to get him interested. He was completely uninterested, and that caused my level of anxiety to skyrocket.

After a long wait, the doctors came and delivered Byron some very serious news. They said that if he didn't have emergency surgery right away, he wouldn't live many more hours. Byron instantly began to second-guess the doctors, telling them they were mistaken and that he just needed medicine and he would be fine. He had me call his parents and my sister, who is a nurse, to get their advice. Although Bryon asked for their advice, he didn't agree with them. Byron had confidence in his regular doctor and insisted that we go home and call his doctor in the morning. After hours of trying to convince him differently, Byron left the hospital against doctors' orders, and somehow, even after I was home and he was in bed for the night, anxiety remained, and I knew something was different this time.

After an hour of watching him struggle, gasp for air, and being unable to communicate normally, I got him back in the chair and took him straight back to the ER. Bryon was pretty angry with me about this decision and kept saying he would be fine. I had a conversation with him about death, and despite Byron's insistence that he was fine, I didn't like what I saw, and it scared me. That was a horrible long night and in the early morning hours, I signed the papers for emergency surgery against Bryon's wishes. I knew he didn't want to stay in the hospital and that he wanted his doctors to treat him, but based on what the doctors were saying and what I was watching, our time was running out. When the hospital staff pushed him into the surgery room on the hospital bed, Byron looked at me with his beautiful but tired blue eyes and said, "Don't let them put a tube down my throat. I love you." Those were the last words he said to me.

Where the Rubber Meets the Road

After surgery, my sister was at the hospital, and his parents were on the way. Byron had been to the hospital many times in the 17 years we were married, but this time I was truly scared. The next two days were excruciating and painful as Byron's worn-out body began to shut down. We had the best doctors around and even though I didn't understand most of what they said; I knew what I saw, and this was not typical for Byron. He could not bounce back like he had done every time before. This was the time he was expecting, the time he had spoken to me about. This was the moment I dreaded and prayed would never come, the time I was determined to avoid for many years to come. Byron was about to be rewarded for his faithfulness to God and his legacy of love here on earth. In my mind, I could hear Byron saying, "Now you have to practice your faith. This is when the rubber meets the road."

Chapter NINE

Lasting Legacy

After some of the most horrific days of my life, I was confronted with the incredible depth of Byron's legacy. Text, calls, visits, and gifts came pouring in from around the world. Byron had lived a life that was extraordinary and now I was face to face with the reality of it all. He touched so many lives and left lasting impressions on people that we knew and some people that we didn't know.

His Legacy in Kenya

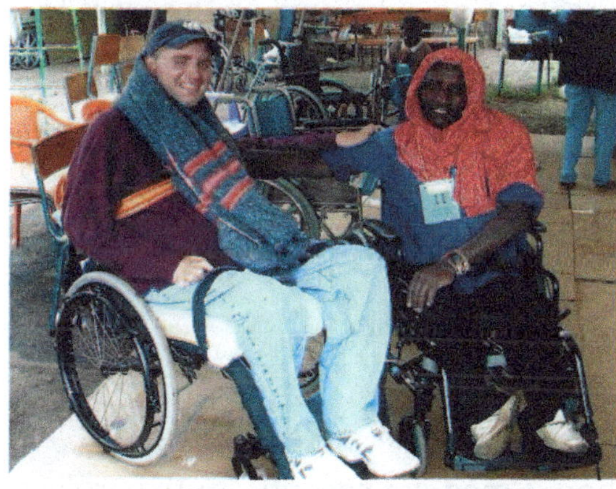

Calls came from pastors and lay people in Kenya who wanted to remember and honor Byron. About a month before Byron died, we received a call from one of our Kenyan friends, named David. During our conversation, he shared that many people visited Nairobi and surrounding cities as tourists or missionaries, but they often leave and are forgotten. David told Byron that the three summers we spent in Kenya had left a lasting impression on his life and the lives of many others. Byron's sacrifice to leave the conveniences of America and go to Kenya as a quadriplegic had opened people's hearts and minds to the plight of people with disabilities. He said that 10 years later, people were still talking about the words Byron shared as he exhorted leaders to include the disabled community in the family of God. Byron's devotion and dependency on God for day-to-day things left a lasting impression that changed that small part of the world.

His testimony and work in Nairobi over 10 years ago had come to life. Families, who had never been accepted before Byron's visits, found churches opening their doors to them. He introduced adults and children with disabilities to their Creator God, who died on the cross for their sins. People who once had misconceptions about the disabled learned to love and embrace these neglected families. God changed lives because of Byron's faithfulness to share the gospel of Jesus Christ on another continent and His legacy in Kenya continues even today.

His Legacy in Prison

In 2013, Byron was invited to speak at Kershaw Correctional Institution, a medium-security South Carolina state prison housing 1500 male inmates. His friend and former driver Gerry was the chaplain there, and they greeted Byron enthusiastically as he entered the prison that day. The men graciously solved the problem of the steps leading up to where he was supposed to speak by lifting him and his power wheelchair onto the chapel platform. The audience was made up of men living together in a community dorm as part of a rehabilitation program. Their focus was on self-discipline, improving personal life skills, and studying finances and business. Also present that day were a dozen chapel workers tasked with organizing programs and managing the movement of inmates taking part in chapel activities. One of the chapel workers was Lester Young, Kershaw's Muslim community leader and life skills class instructor. Lester had served 20 years of a life sentence and had been denied parole six months prior to meeting Byron. Being denied parole is a hard pill to swallow, especially after spending so many years behind bars.

Chaplain Gerry Potoka remembers that day:

"Byron began his presentation by stating that he understood what it was like to be in prison. He said that the inmates were behind the prison walls, but as a quadriplegic, he was in prison in his wheelchair. He told the men that they might one day get out of their prison, but he would never get out of his, and then he said, "But let me tell you how good God is to me in this chair." Byron talked about his unique ability to minister to thousands of people who had been similarly disabled by accidents or birth defects. He told them how he was able to work full time with Joni & Friends, a ministry that brings hope and care to families struggling with a variety of illnesses or tragic mishaps. Byron shared his story about being able to travel

halfway around the world to assist people with disabilities in Kenya, Africa."

After listening to Byron speak that day, Lester told Chaplain Potoka that he now understood why he didn't make parole. He was supposed to meet Byron and hear his story. Byron's story gave Lester a whole new purpose for living and changed his perspective on prison and suffering. Lester later wrote a book called The Five Stages of Incarceration helping inmates work through denial, anger, victimization, forgiveness, and transformation.

Byron's life had that effect on people. His story encouraged others to change their story. He didn't deny his personal struggles with his own physical condition, but chose to live life on a higher plane, in the right relationship with God, and in joyful ministry and service to others.

His Legacy in Honduras

Byron was blessed to have all kinds of supplies and equipment that helped him complete his daily tasks. He had a power wheelchair he used daily, as well as a shower chair, a manual chair he used when we traveled overseas, braces, medical supplies, and all kinds of pillows and cushions. One of Byron's best friends, Mary, was involved with a ministry that served a small community in Honduras. Shortly after Byron died, the ministry discovered a young man named Waltercito, who had significant cognitive and physical disabilities. The family had very few resources, and Waltercito spent most of his life laying flat on a bed or couch. He was over 20 years old

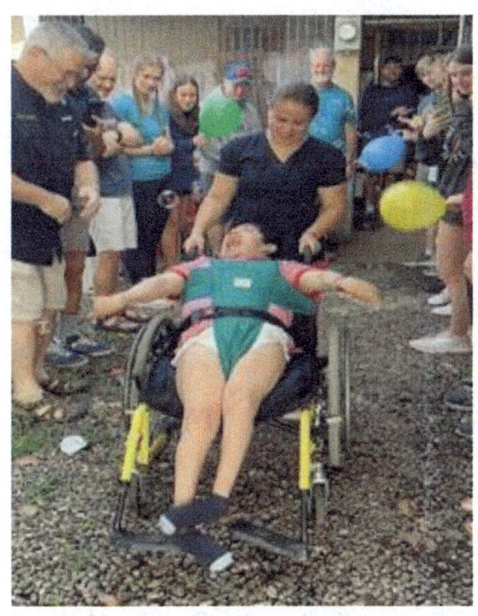

and had never sat up in a chair. The team that Mary worked with transported Byron's manual wheelchair to Honduras and gave Waltercito and his family the gift of mobility! The team built a ramp into his house and Waltercito was able to roll out of his house for the first time in his life! What a blessing it was to make that connection and see Byron's yellow chair change a stranger's life.

His Legacy Throughout North Carolina

In July 2023, my Aunt Jan had to use special transportation when she was transferred from a hospital in Matthews to a rehabilitation facility in Concord. This incident became another God story. Aunt Jan was sitting in a manual wheelchair in a special transportation van with her Bible on her lap. The driver began to talk to Aunt Jan about her Bible and church. The conversation led to the driver telling Jan that she wasn't attending church right now, but in the past she had attended a church in Charlotte that had a disability ministry. She shared she had a disabled son and described how difficult it was to find a church that could meet his needs and also allow her to attend a service. As the lady continued her story, she mentioned an experience she had with a quadriplegic man who ran a disability ministry. She said the man had joy in his eyes, and he always made her and her son feel loved and welcome. She shared how different the church was when he was there to help them and how rare it was to find a place with that loving feeling of acceptance and genuine kindness. The man was Byron.

His Legacy at Family Camp

Over the years, Byron spent many summers with Joni and Friends in the NC mountains serving families with disabilities at the annual JAF Family Retreats. During the Family Retreats, Byron would take part in various activities like wheelchair races, whitewater rafting, and Bible studies. He led devotions and shared Jesus with entire families that were affected by disabilities.

In 2014, Byron was invited to be the camp pastor for a recently formed family retreat in Tennessee, called Camp Celebrate. The camp allowed people with disabilities and their families to enjoy a time to be refreshed and encouraged in a fun atmosphere. Parents could have a break as their children were cared for by volunteers selected to meet the needs of the disabled. Byron partnered with Ms. Darlene, the camp director, developing multiple sermons for the adults and parents that attended the retreat. He took this responsibility seriously, as he felt his calling was to speak to the heart of families that loved someone with a disability. Many welcomed Byron's wisdom as he brought his unique perspective of having experienced life both with and without a disability. Byron built relationships with moms, dad, caregivers, and campers and showed them Jesus. He spoke truth to them from his heart and from the word of God. He encouraged them to take chances and put their faith in Jesus. Byron served as camp pastor for 7 years, and his legacy lives on through the many hearts that were influenced by his faith, devotion, and dependency on God.

His Legacy of Family and Friends

After our life on earth is over, our legacy is the only thing we leave behind. Over the past 2 years, I have heard Byron's legacy recounted to me by those who knew him well and those who only met him a few times. Some say, "He always greeted me with a smile on his face. He made me feel at home and welcome every time we spoke. He seemed like he had joy from within." Others said, "He was effortlessly funny, especially leading VBS and teaching the kids on Sunday mornings. His high fives with his "broken hands" were priceless." Many of the churchgoers remember Byron on Sunday mornings with his "genuine smile from the top of the stairs at church." My favorite description of him was from someone who mentioned that "He was the type of man that called just to check on me and my family and see how we were doing even when he needed nothing. He was genuine, real, and had peace that passed all understanding."

Byron had fun, made jokes, listened more than he talked, and saw the best in people. He lived his life dependent on Christ to meet his daily needs. He never gave up and never doubted where his help came from. We will forever carry Byron's legacy in our lives as we try to finish our race on earth by pursuing Jesus and looking for opportunities to love people in His name.

Holding the Door to Heaven

Early in our dating life, I distinctly remember one night when Byron and I were rolling and walking as we headed into a store. When I approached the large sliding door, Byron yelled, "Stop! Wait!" I abruptly turned towards him as he said, "wait right there." He rolled up to the door and, as the door opened automatically, he proudly said, "Now you can go in. I opened the door for you." I just smiled and loved him even more. Now, whenever I walk through an electric door, my heart smiles as I think of the way Byron always put me first and made me feel special. He has gone through the door of heaven before me, but one day I will hear him say "wait right there" as he opens the door for me and welcomes me home.

Made in the USA
Monee, IL
12 April 2024

56863320R00046